More About The Huguenots: A Review Of Prof. William Gammell's Lecture On "the Huguenots And The Edict Of Nantes...

William Stang (Bishop)

PREFACE.

On the twenty-second day of October of the past year the descendants of the Huguenots in several parts of this country celebrated the two hundreth anniversary of the revocation of the Edict of Nantes. In many places the celebration was made the occasion of discourses on the Church of Rome, her religious intolerance, etc. In the city of Providence the event was commemorated in a very interesting and polished lecture by Prof. William Gammell, the President of the Rhode Island Historical Society, which has since appeared in print.

Professor Gammell is undoubtedly an able and well-meaning man. His lecture is comparatively free from the vituperations and invectives which are usually flung by Protestants against the Catholics of France. There is a marked difference between it and the paper read at a subsequent meeting of the Society, wherein a deal of sentimental fiction and ungentle declamation are meant to inspire horror of "Romanist fanaticism and cruelty." Yet even Prof. Gammell so often, unintentionally no doubt, misrepresents and omits facts that we cannot in the compass of a small pamphlet go over his errors point by point; we will endeavor to point them out, as much in detail as we may, by a general review of his paper.

On many grave questions the learned Professor is rather non-committal. Thus, for instance, he is careful not to attribute the Massacre of St. Bartholomew to the Church of Rome, yet he makes Pope "Gregory the XIII. and the College of Cardinals" go "in procession to church after church" in thanksgiving for the slaughter of the Huguenots.

By a calm and clear statement of historical facts we hope to throw some light on this already much-ventilated subject of the Huguenots.

CHAPTER I.

HISTORICAL NOTES ON THE HUGUENOTS.

The struggle of Protestantism for recognition in France, though called religious, was essentially political and had little to do with religion itself. The Huguenots had "made themselves," as Prof. Gammell admits, "a separate political body— framed in accordance with the theories of Calvin." They formed in the very heart of France a revolutionary party, dangerous, nay, destructive to throne and altar; their wars were distinctively civil wars.

What Macauley says of the Reformation in general, can be applied to Calvinism in France: "The only event in modern times which can be properly compared with the Reformation, is the French revolution." *

Princes, especially of the house of Navarre, became the frends and defenders of Calvinism for political purposes, chiefly in opposition to the reigning influence of the powerful dukes of Guise.

Atrocities of the most revolting nature were committed on both sides; but we must remember that the Huguenots were the offenders and aggressors; that, in many cases, the Catholic party acted in self-defense; that, at that time, according to the common law of Europe, heresy was a civil crime. Moreover, in whatever country Protestantism had, at that time, gained ascendancy, it cruelly persecuted and oppressed the Catholic religion. The treatment of their Catholic brethren in neighboring Protestant countries had so terrified

* Miscell., II.

French Catholics that they sought to avert, as far as lay in their power, a like calamity from their own country.

As early as 1525, the Calvinists or Huguenots, in the city of Meaux, desecrated statues of the saints, defied the lawful authorities, and exasperated the people. Their ringleader was arrested by the civil authorities, convicted and suffered the then not uncommon death-penalty throughout Europe of burning at the stake.

In 1528, a party of Huguenots, in the city of Paris, attacked and mutilated a public statue of the Virgin and Child. This public outrage aroused general indignation against them.

It should not be forgotten that, at this time, France was a country intensely Catholic, although its court was corrupt.

Francis I., an unprincipled, licentious, tyrannical and treacherous monarch, leagued himself with the Turks, the hereditary enemy of Christian civilization ; he supported the Protestants of Germany, while he persecuted the Protestants of France, because it served his purpose. But taken all in all, the priests and people of France were instinctively opposed to the introduction of any new heresy. Prof. Gammell's assertion that "the relations of the Gallican church and the Papacy had been disturbed" is by no means at one with the report of Heynes and Mont to their royal master, Henry VIII., (sent from France on the 8th of August, 1535), stating the French clergy to be "wholli dedicat to the Bishop of Rome, and highly estimeth his authorite." *

The Huguenots daily grew in impudence towards the Old Church. The emblem of the Redemption, a statue of the Virgin or any sacred image would fill them with fury, and lead them to atrocious profanations. On October 18, 1535,

* State Papers, under Henry VIII.; see Vol. VII.

they posted on the walls of the Louvre, and the doors of the King's chamber even, copies of a villainous pamphlet, entitled "True Articles on the horrible and great Abuses of the Popish Mass."

It is difficult for a Protestant to imagine the feelings of indignation which such a pamphlet would naturally arouse in the hearts of Catholics who believe in Christ's real presence in the Eucharist; to conceive an adequate idea of their exasperation forced to look upon outrages and blasphemous deeds against the Virgin Mary, the Mother of Christ, whom they regard as the masterpiece of creation, as the perfect type and "example of all womanhood,"* as the "defense of many truths, and the grace and smiling light of every devotion;" † whose very name sunshines the Catholic heart with joy and hope.

> "The name
> Of that fair Flower, whom duly I invoke
> Both morn and eve.
>
> Here is the Rose
> Wherein the Word Divine was made incarnate."‡

Led on by their theologians and preachers, the Huguenots formed a conspiracy against the life of the King and the family of Guise (1560), known as the conspiracy of Amboise, which was timely discovered.§ A year before, at a general synod, held in Paris, the Calvinists decreed "that all heretics should be put to death."‖ They were not satisfied with religious equality; they would be content only with the

* Longfellow; Golden Legend.
† Cardinal Newman's Discourses to Mixed Congregations.
‡ Dante; Paradise, XXIII.
§ Bossuet, Hist. des variat, X, 23.
‖ Cf. Alzog's Church History, III, 272.

destruction of the Catholic Church in France. Excited by their preachers to the wildest fanaticism, they attempted to root out the Catholic religion.

At Rouen they destroyed the sepulchral monuments of the Norman dukes; they threw the bones of St. Irenaeus and St. Martin into the river Seine, and pulled down the statue of the Virgin of Orleans. Prince Condé struck coins from golden and silver Church vessels, and had cannon cast from consecrated bells, and thus untuned the hallowed voice of prayer into the lugubrious boom of war. Scarcely a monument of art escaped the fury of the Huguenots.* Even Dr. Fisher admits that their iconoclastic fury was attended with great destruction of monuments of art and profanations of sepulchres.†

They also set fire to many celebrated libraries; amongst them the famous library of Cluny, containing about six thousand precious manuscripts. ‡

In the Dauphiné alone, the Huguenots burnt down nine hundred towns and villages.

The Huguenots committed their worst deeds in the little kingdom of Bearn, under the cruel Jane d'Albret, where by fire they destroyed three hundred Catholic churches; they turned into blackened ruins not less than eight hundred churches in France, of which fifty were cathedrals. The magnificent cathedral of Beziers served as a stable for their horses.§

Their acts of destruction were as a rule accompanied by bloodshed and murder. In Sully, Coligny slaughtered thirty-

---

* Janssen, Geschichte des deutschen Volkes, IV. 243.

† History of the Reformation, p. 268.

‡ Janssen, l. c.

§ Cf. Dr. Brueck; Kirchengeschichte, p. 628.

five priests ; in Pithiviers he ordered all the priests to be destroyed.* At the Council of Trent, the Cardinal of Lorraine reported three thousand persons of different religious orders to have been murdered by the Huguenots within a few months.†

Briquemont, a Huguenot leader, wore a necklace made of the ears of murdered priests.‡ Count Montgomery caused the slaughter of three thousand Catholics at Orthèz. In the Dauphiné, Baron des Adrets amused himself by forcing Catholics to jump from a precipice onto the pikes of Huguenot soldiers, and had his children wash their hands in the blood of the slain. §

Despite these many cruelties, Prof. Gammell is unable to give us more than " one lamentable instance " of Huguenot atrocity, which he extenuatingly calls "a solitary exception to the general conduct of their campaigns."

One of the darkest pages in the history of the Huguenots is that on which is written the murder of Francis of Guise, whom Sismondi calls "a great man, and one of the most virtuous and religious men that France ever possessed." His enemies were for a long time conspiring against his life, and Coligny and Beza were the chief actors in the conspiracy. Francis of Guise was of a most generous and high-minded character. At Rouen a Calvanist, named Bonneguard, fired at the duke and missed him. Bonneguard was

---

* Bossuet, Hist. des variat, X., 52.

† Cf. Janssen, l. c. An old book, printed at Antwerp in 1588, contains many illustrations of the tortures used by Calvinists in the execution of monks and priests : " Theatrum crudelitatum Haereticorum nostri temporis."

‡ See Brueck, l. c.

§ Ibidem ; also Bossuet, Hist. des variat, X.

2

brought before the duke, who with his usual serenity asked his would-be murderer whether he had wronged him that he should attempt his life. The Huguenot coolly replied: "No; but you are the enemy of *the* religion which justifies me in killing you." "My religion," the duke calmly said, "teaches me to forgive you. Judge from this which of the two is the right one." The last words of the dying duke were of pardon for his murderers.

Over and above their acts of cruelty and vandalism, a stigma will forever attach to the Huguenot leaders as traitors to their country. Coligny and Condé raised troops in England and the Protestant parts of Germany to assist them against their own countrymen. By the treaty of September 20, 1562, the Huguenots gave Havre to Queen Elizabeth, and promised her Calais in return for assistance in their rebellion. The bulk of the rebel army, however, was composed of German Protestant mercenaries, who, ever since the Reformation, were the most venal men in Europe; selling their services to Catholic and Protestant powers indiscriminately. No longer united by the bond of a common faith, the mighty German empire was crumbling to pieces; state warred against state; Protestant princes lent their swords to whomsoever gave highest wage. The Huguenots were not everywhere rich, and so in several places these German soldiers were invited to pay themselves in plunder and pillage, and Coligny energetically proposed that they should live at the cost of the papists. These Germans, however, made no religious distinction among their victims, but mercilessly committed such horrible cruelties against friend and foe as to deserve the appellation of "German Barbarians."[*]

On the 23d of August, 1572, the Huguenots assembled in

[*] Janssen, l. c., pp. 245, 246.

Paris, concerted a plan to take possession of the Louvre on the day following, to kill the royal family, and proclaim Henry of Navarre King of France.* The news of this plot reached the royal palace on the same day, and the "intriguing" and godless Catherine de Medicis persuaded her son to command the horrible massacre of St. Bartholomew's day.

When Gregory XIII. received the tidings of the sudden and successful suppression of a Calvanist conspiracy against the Court of France, he congratulated King Charles IX. on the event. "These congratulations," as Dr. Alzog well observes, "are of precisely the same character as the felicitations addressed by European sovereigns to one of their royal cousins upon his escape and preservation from some direful calamity, and being consonant with usage among princes, need excite no surprise, much less the affected horror with which dishonest and sentimental writers are accustomed to speak of them."†

On the 5th of September a "Te Deum" was sung in the Church of San Marco, at Rome, in thanksgiving for the preservation of the royal family and of the Catholic religion in France, and three days after a solemn service was held in the French church at Rome. When the true story of the bloody deed with its disgusting details was presented to the Pope, he sincerely grieved over the bloodshed, and "to a nobleman expressed his horror at the deed, even with tears."‡

Both the Catholics and the Protestants of Europe abhorred the detestable slaughter ; the German Lutherans alone thought differently, and regarded the massacre as a just revenge of Almighty God on the Huguenots.§

* Ibidem, p. 318.

† Church History, III. 279.

‡ See Hergenroether; Church and State, II. 379.

§ Brueck, Kirchengeschichte, p. 632.

The number of victims in the massacre of St. Bartholomew is generally exaggerated. According to an old register, kept in the Hotel de Ville at Paris, the grave-diggers of Paris buried eleven hundred bodies. About two thousand people were killed in the provinces.* The "martyrology" of the Huguenots gives the names of seven hundred and eighty-six who perished in the sanguinary drama.

The famous Edict of Nantes granted full religious freedom to all Calvinists in France, and also demanded the free exercise of the Catholic religion in those places where it had been violently suppressed by the Huguenots.

But neither at Bearn nor in the fortified places did the Huguenots comply with the demands of the Edict; they stubbornly refused to grant religious toleration to their Catholic fellow-citizens. Buckle, the Protestant historian, remarks: "The Protestants soon learned to despise the Edict of Nantes, by which their liberties were secured, and proceeded to rob and murder that very party to which they owed a toleration, which had been reluctantly conceded by the prejudices (?) of the age."†

We have nothing to say in defense of the dreadful dragonade which the despotic Louis XIV. attempted in order to force conversion upon the Huguenots. The Church is not to blame for the crimes of a disobedient son; and Louis XIV. disregarded her commands. The Holy See, as a matter of course, condemned the dragonade, and Pope Innocent XI. strove through his nuncio d'Adda's influence with King James II. of England to move Louis XIV. to milder measures towards the Huguenots.‡ Pope Clement XI. remarked

* Wetzer and Welte, Kirchenlexicon, II. 934.
† History of Civilization in England.
‡ See Brueck, l. c.

about compelling Huguenots into the Church: "Christ never used such means; we must lead people to the Church and not drag them in."*

The number of Huguenots who emigrated is given, by Aubineau, as sixty-eight thousand."†

During the formidable wars and riots of the Huguenots, Catholic bishops exerted their influence and authority to quell the furious excitement of their Catholic people against Protestants. The noble bishop of Lisieux sheltered the Huguenots in his diocese against State persecution, and justified his protection of them in these memorable words: "It is the duty of the good shepherd to lay down his life for his sheep; not to let them be slaughtered before his face. These are my sheep, though they have gone astray; and I am resolved to run all hazards in the protecting them."‡

The kind and persuasive efforts of the Catholic clergy, coupled with true zeal and charity, brought many deluded and misguided Huguenots back to the fold of Christ.

* Cf. Doellinger; Kirche und Kirchen, (Introduction.)
† De la revocation de l'édict de Nantes. Paris, 1875.
‡ Cf. Spalding; History of the Reformation, II.

CHAPTER II.

In the light of impartial history it is very difficult to dis-
cover in the character of the heroes of Calvinism any of the
qualities which should mark the champions and promoters of
faith and religion. However well-meaning, Prof. Gammell
really does not give the descendants of the Huguenots a cor-
rect idea of their "heroic" ancestors, as we shall briefly
show by passing them in review.

John Calvin is justly regarded as the father of the Huguenots, "as their patriarch and chief." Trained in the great
Catholic school of the Sorbonne, he had attracted attention
by his distinguished scholarship and erudition. But, as
Alzog appropriately remarks, "cleverness and study cannot
compensate for bad character and loose morals, and both the
character and the morals of Calvin were infamous."* Though
wielding a classical pen, Calvin's language was frequently as
coarse and vulgar as that of Martin Luther. As Dr. Fisher
remarks, Calvin was "occasionally so carried away by gusts
of passion, that he lost all self-control."† The illustrious
Yale Professor, however, merges too closely the character of
Calvin and that of the Saxon Reformer. For, as Bossuet
observes, Calvin's cruel and iniquitous executions were not,
"as in the case of Luther, the effect of hasty impulse or
uncontrollable bursts of anger, but the result of cool, calcu-

* Church History, III. 144.
† History of the Reformation, 204.

lating and unfeeling malignity, that have left a stain upon the memory of the French Reformer which will never be effaced."*

His vindictive fury was never appeased; it followed his adversary beyond the grave. A celebrated scholar of the age, Pighius, had opposed the teachings of Calvin; the courteous John was not called upon to write his epitaph; his gentle, cold soul knew for him no other appellation than "dead dog."

The character of Calvin seems to be better known to the citizens of Geneva than to many of our American friends; for, twenty-two years ago, they refused to celebrate the third centennial of Calvin's death, and put up posters proclaiming the capital sentences against Servetus and Berthilier.†

Palissy the Potter undoubtedly was, as described by Prof. Gammell, a skillful clay enameller, and for his time well up in geology, but as to his religion, he appears to us a veritable conundrum. He must have been a "simple gospeller," indeed; for he was "without church;" and certainly "a man of extraordinary genius," since he was of "heroic faith" "without a creed."

James Lefévre, better known as the humanist, Faber Sta-pulensis, was a great biblical scholar; at first he welcomed Luther's cry for a Reformation, but within the Church, never dreaming of a separation therefrom. He translated the Latin Bible into French, but failed to obtain for his version the approbation of the Sarbonne doctors, with whom he was often at odds. The Belgian theologians, however, approved

* Hist. des variat. IX.

† The Augsburger Allegem. Zeitung, of June 2, 1864, has this item: Calvin's latest descendant, a respectable and virtuous citizen of Noyen, has just returned to the bosom of that Church from which his ancestor apostatized so shamefully.

it. Revised by Nicholas de Leuze and other Louvain doctors, Lefévre's version became the French Catholic Bible for a hundred years. Of a "mystical vein,"[*] Lefévre was fond of startling ideas, and was besides somewhat pugnacious. In private life, he was a man of spotless character, full of piety and zeal, honest and frank. He died a devout Roman Catholic.[†] It is hardly fair to reckon him among the leaders of French Calvinism.

William Farel is described by Erasmus as "the most arrogant, abusive and shameless man he had ever met with."[‡] His vile and wild invectives drew down upon him the wrath of the Council of Geneva, who forbade him to preach within the limits of the "Reformed" city.

Briçonnet, "the kind-hearted bishop" of Meaux, in the beginning credited the "Reformers" with purely religious motives; but he no sooner discovered their aims than he straightway renounced any further communion with them.

Prof. Gammell assures us that, besides men of learning, French Protestantism "early numbered among its votaries men and women of rank, officers of distinction in the service of the country, and even princes of the royal blood." In the course of his lecture, Mr. Gammell gives us the names of some of these distinguished votaries. "A more remark-

---

[*] Fisher, l. c., p. 244.

[†] See the article in Wetzer & Welte, III. 872-874.

[‡] Fisher, l. c., p. 210.—Sister Jeanne de Jussie has left a curious account of Farel's personal attractions: "In the month of October (1532) there came to Geneva a mean-looking, wretched, little preacher called Maitre Guillaume, shabby in his person, with a vulgar face, a narrow forehead, a pale but sunburnt complexion, and a chin on which grew two or three tufts of red and tangled beard." (Quoted in the Catholic World, XXVII., 781.

able promoter of the new faith" than the translators of the Bible and the preachers, "appeared in the person of Queen Margaret of Valois, the sister of Francis I., "King of France."

Now, I take it for certain that no member of the Rhode Island Historical Society would have his daughter form the acquaintance of this "remarkable promoter of the new faith," for Margaret of Valois' ideas of propriety would be condemned by every New England lady. Without going into unsavory details, suffice it to say that the Queen of Navarre is the authoress of the ill-famed "Heptameron."

"Jane d'Albret, a Protestant alike by birth and by choice and a champion of the Protestant faith," is the other of the two "women of rank" and of the "royal blood" mentioned by the Professor.* Jane d'Albret, wife of Anthony of Bourbon, went so far in her zeal for the "new faith" that in her little kingdom of Bearn she put all Catholics out of office, expelled all Catholic priests and interdicted every form of Catholic worship.† A wild fanatisism had made her cruel and despotic.

Prince Condé, a leader of the early Huguenots, has left a character in history which honest men will hesitate to call reputable. A faithless husband, he broke the heart of his wife ;‡ by conspiring against his sovereign and negotiating with foreign powers against his own country, he was often guilty of the most flagrant high-treason. Queen Elizabeth

---

* Prof. Gammell has omitted the name of another "woman of rank" and "promoter of the new faith," Ann Pisseleu, the profligate mistress of Francis I.

† Cf. Brueck, p. 625.

‡ Janssen, l. c., p. 245.

of England called Condé for breach of promise "a traitor and a scoundrel, only fit to be flung to the dogs."*

The centre and soul of the Huguenot struggle in the beginning of the latter half of the sixteenth century was Admiral Coligny, the Robespierre of the Protestant revolution in France. A traitor to his king and country, he seemed infuriated with burning hatred against his country's religion, and in fact against everything Catholic. The dream of his life and the object of all his great political movements was the destruction of Catholic Spain.† This explains why Philip II. laughed—if he did laugh, as Prof. Gammell tells us—when he receved the tidings of the Admiral's death. This Coligny was a sour and gloomy hypocrite who would strike off the hand of a soldier for the sin of cursing, while in his own heart he was brooding the murder of the noblest blood of France. He plotted, and by the hand of John Poltrot, whom he had provided with the means of his dastardly deed, accomplished the assassination of Francis of Guise, the bravest soldier of France.‡

*Cf. Kervyn de Lettenhove; Les Huguenots et les Gueux, I., 140
† See proofs apud Janssen, N. 310.
‡ Ibidem, p. 244.

CHAPTER III.

"The Reformation demanded that the Scriptures be given to the human race for whom they were designed, instead of being confined to the priests alone." Thus the Professor. In the very next sentence, by way of contradiction it would seem, he continues: "The invention of printing had just made the Bible an accessible book to all who could read, and multitudes everywhere were searching for its hitherto unknown teachings and promises." The invention of printing came eighty years before the Reformation. The religious, or better, the Catholic world, for Protestantism was not, looked upon the new discovery as a heavenly gift, a special Providential revelation. Catholic prelates* called it a "divine art," "a holy art," "a heavenly benefit," etc. The first book printed was a Latin Bible. Through this art, the Professor remarks, the Bible was made "an accessible book to all;" why then should the Reformers after eighty years demand "that it should be given to the human race?" However, we presume that this is but a chronological slip; we can come at the Professor's meaning; he has been imposed upon by the old historical falsehood, and has added another to its almost countless utterances, that the Bible was inaccessible to the people before the Reformation.

Better than three hundred and fifty years ago, the greatest and most celebrated scholar in England, Sir Thomas

* Archbishop Birthold of Mentz, Bishop John of Aleria, Archbishop Nicholas of Siponto, etc.

More, "whose memory lives in every cultivated bosom,"* refuted this error; and here are his own words: "I have shewed you that the clergy keep no Bibles from the laity that can no more but their mother tongue, but such translations as be either not yet approved for good or such as be already reproved for naught, as Wickliffe's was. For as for old ones that were before Wickliffe's days, they remained lawful & be in some folks' hands." And again: "The hole Byble was, long before Wickliffe's dayes, by vertuous & wel learned men, translated into the English tong, & by good & godly people, with devotion & soberness, wel & reverently red."†

What was true of England at that time could be more strictly said of other countries. In the preface to the first separate edition of the New Testament, published in 1475, the printer says: "It is the general cry that every believer who professes to have any knowledge of letters is bound to have an acquaintance with the Holy Scriptures, and more particularly with that part of the Bible called the New Testament."‡

Half a century before Palissy the Potter peddled it, the New Testament was in circulation.

Up to the year 1500 the Vulgate had been printed not less than a hundred times. Latin was then a truly catholic language, almost universally known and spoken; so much so, that all who could read at all, could understand it.

There were fifteen versions in High German of the Complete Bible, and five in Low German, before Martin Luther

* Dibdin's Bibliomania, p. 541.

† Blunt, History of the Reformation, I. 505.—Wiseman, Principal Doctrines, I. p. 57.

‡ Timperley's Dictionary of Printing, p. 158.

began to translate *his* Bible. In fact the Bible was translated and *printed* in almost every European language.*

That the Holy Scriptures were translated and known in France before the Calvinist "gospellers" overran the country, will be evident from the following facts : The Psalter was printed in French in 1474; the Bible of Julien (complete) in or about 1478; several books of the Old Testament in 1482; the edition of Menand in 1484; the complete Bible translated by de Rely, and printed in two folios, at Paris by Verard, (it appeared in several editions); the Apocalypse in 1502; the Epistles of St. Paul in 1507; the Psalms in 1513.

The author of a very solid and erudite work, "the History of the Reformation of the Church of England," Rev. J. H. Blunt, a Protestant clergyman, candidly confesses :† "There has been much wild and foolish writing about the scarcity of the Bible in the ages preceding the Reformation. The facts are that the clergy and monks were daily reading large portions of the Bible, and had them stored up in their memory by constant recitation ; that they made free use of Holy Scripture in preaching, so that even a modern Bible-reader is astonished at the number of quotations and references contained in mediæval sermons ; that countless copies of the Bible were written out by the surprising industry of cloistered scribes ; that many glosses or commentaries were written which are still seen to be full of pious and wise thoughts ; that all laymen who could read were, as a rule, provided with their gospels, their psalter, or other devotional portions of the Bible. Men did, in fact, take a vast amount of trouble with respect to the production of copies of the Holy Scriptures,

* Wetzer and Welte, Kirchenlexicon. (See Appendix.)

† See Vol. II., p. 501.

and accomplished by head, hands and heart what is now chiefly done by paid workmen and machinery. The clergy studied the word of God and made it known to the laity; and those few among the laity who could read had abundant opportunity of reading the Bible, either in Latin or in English, up to the Reformation period."

Fortescue says of the judges of his time*—half a century before the Reformation—that they spent the afternoon "in the study of the laws, reading of the Holy Scriptures, and other innocent amusements." Pearce, a Protestant author, remarks:"† It deserves notice that at periods anterior to the Reformation the Holy Scriptures were studied in the Inns of the Court—a fact which had been overlooked by those who have supposed that prior to that era the sacred volume was altogether a 'sealed book' to the laity."

The Catholic believes all those things which God has revealed, and his Church teaches. His rule of faith is the Church's infallible interpretation of revealed truth as handed down in the Bible and by tradition. Christ appointed his Church to be the teacher of all mankind;‡ to enable her to fulfill her mission He promised her the assistance of the Paraclete forever.§

The Church, fully organized, exercised her divine rights on earth before a word of the New Testament was written. St. Matthew wrote the first words of the New Testament six years after Christ's ascension. Christ did not commission His Apostles to write, but to preach,‖—nor did the Apostles

* De Laudibus Legum Angliæ, p. 126.
† History of the Inns of Court and Chancery; London, 1848.
‡ Matth. xxviii., 18-20.
§ John, xiv., 16.
‖ Mark, xvi., 15; Matth. xxviii., 19.

ever assert that the Epistles and Gospels contained all that Christ had done and taught; they maintained the very contrary: "Many other signs also did Jesus in the sight of His disciples which are not written in this book;"* and St. Paul expressly exhorts the Thessalonians :† "Stand fast and hold the *traditions* which you have learned, whether by *word* or by our Epistle."

The Catholic Church alone received the truth of Scripture and of Tradition from the Apostles; we are compelled to look to her as "the pillar and ground of truth,"‡ for all the assurance we have of their divine origin; she alone can give us the authentic Bible. Wherefore the great St. Augustine says :§ "I should not believe the Gospels, unless the authority of the Church moved me thereto."

The Infallible Church guides the believer through the obscure parts of the Scriptures; she gives life to the dead volume; she opens to him the hidden treasures of its mysterious pages.

The Bible is full of difficulties and obscurities not only for the ignorant and stupid, but for the most learned and talented. Of the Epistles of St. Paul, St. Peter says there are in them‖ "certain things hard to be understood, which the unlearned and unstable wrest to their own destruction." Hence, whenever left to private interpretation the Bible has been blasphemously distorted into absurdities and invoked to shield error and vice. "Neither have heretics," St. Augustine writes,¶ "and certain perverse doctrines, which

* John xx., 30.
† 2 Thess., ii., 14.
‡ 1 Tim., iii., 15.
§ Contra Ep. Fund., c. 5.
‖ II. Pet., iii., 16.
¶ Tract. 18 in Joan. n. 1.

ensnare souls and cast them headlong into hell, sprung up, but by the good Scriptures being ill-understood, and what is therein badly understood is rashly and boldly asserted."

Scarcely had Luther proclaimed his doctrine on private judgment and private interpretation of the Bible, than his followers branched out into a variety of religious opinions different from those of their "apostle," so that the "Reformer" in his letter to the Christians of Antwerp exclaimed with bitterness:* "One rejects baptism; another the Eucharist; another constructs a new world between the present and that which will arise after the last judgment; some deny the divinity of Christ. One says this; the other that; *there are as many sects as there are heads.* Everybody imagines himself inspired by the Holy Ghost and wants to be a prophet."

Janssen, the historian, relates† some practical Scripture interpretations of Luther's followers, about the year 1524. In St. Gall a number of men suddenly awoke to the significance of the divine precept, "Go into the whole world and preach the Gospel." Accordingly they met in the town, and by mutual agreement rushed through the city-gates toward the four quarters of the earth. In Appenzell twelve thousand persons assembled according to the text: "Do not care of what you shall eat," and abstained from food until hunger compelled them to disperse. Some climbed upon the roofs of houses and preached from their exalted stations because Christ had said: "That which you hear in the ear, preach ye upon the house-tops." Others again threw the Bible into the fire according to their interpretation of the divine word: "The letter killeth; the spirit vivifieth."

* De Wette, III., 61.

† Geschehte des deutschen Volkes, II., 386. See also Stang's Life of Luther, p. 54.

At all times and in all places, the Church has practically shown her love and reverence for the written Word of God,— a love and reverence equal to that she has for the Word Incarnate.

For centuries she kept continually thousands of learned and holy men engaged in translating and transcribing the Bible in letters of gold, on costly parchment; she had it bound in covers that withstood the gnawing tooth of time. No sooner was printing invented than she employed it in her sacred service, chiefly for the spreading of the Word of God. And while she always guards against lawless and perverted translations, against arbitrary and impious interpretations of the Bible, jealously keeping watch over her sacred trust, she cherishes it lovingly, interprets it infallibly, and entreats her children in the words of the Immortal Dante :

> " Be ye more staid,
> O Christians ! not, like feathers, by each wind
> Removable ; nor think to cleanse yourselves
> In every water.   Either testament,
> The old and new, is yours ; and for your guide,
> The shepherd of the Church.   Let this suffice
> To save you.   When by evil lust enticed,
> Remember ye be men, not senseless beasts ;
> Nor let the Jew that dwelleth in your streets,
> Hold you in mockery.   Be not as the lamb,
> That, fickle wanton, leaves its mother's milk,
> To dally with itself in idle play."
>
> Paradise, V., 73-85.

4

CHAPTER IV.

CATHOLIC INTOLERANCE AND PROTESTANT TOLERATION.

Christ came on earth to found a kingdom, to establish a church.* He endowed His Church with absolute authority ;† He made her the mouth-piece of Infallible truth.‡ He constituted only one church, one body under a visible head, a single flock under one shepherd.§ He prayed to His heavenly Father for the unity of His Church.‖

In his letter to the Ephesians, St. Paul says : " One body and one spirit . . . . one Lord, one faith, one baptism."¶

To the Church this unity of faith is essential ; wherefore St. Paul entreats the Corinthians : "I beseech you, brethren by the name of our Lord Jesus Christ, that you all speak the same thing, and that there be no schisms among you ; but that you be perfect in the same mind, and in the same judgment."**

There is no room for private judgment in matters of revealed truth. "If any one preach to you a gospel besides that which you have received, let him be anathema."††

* Matth. xvi., 18.
† Luke x., 16.
‡ Matth. xxviii., 20.
§ Ephes. i., 10; St. John x., 16.
‖ John xvii., 20-22.
¶ Ephes. iv., 4.
** I. Cor. i., 10.
†† Gal. i., 9.

The Roman Catholic Church knows herself to be the only true Church of Christ, and as such she needs must cherish and defend her unity. "Any ecclasiastical body," remarks the celebrated canonist Walter,* "conscious of being the depository of absolute objective truth, and of holding the eternal destinies of the whole human race, must consider itself the only true Church, and all other creeds differing from it as more or less in error. Therefore this Church must consider herself deputed to resist and refute all such creeds, and thereby to cause the true doctrine to prevail."

Truth is one and simple; abhorring error, it is necessarily intolerant. Man is not free to believe error. A man who would insist that he is at liberty to believe that two and two make five, would be set down as a fool.

The Catholic Church, the depository of divine truth, abhors error; she must regard, with the Apostle of Christ,† offenses against truth, against religion (for religion is truth), especially apostasy and heresy, as crimes against God Himself.

The Catholic Church is the spouse of Christ and admits of no rival. "The spouse of Christ," St. Cyprian writes, in the third century, (de unit. eccl.), "cannot become adulterate; she is undefiled and chaste. She owns but one home; with spotless purity, she regards the sanctity of one chamber. She keeps us for God; she appoints unto the kingdom the sons she has borne. Whosoever, having separated from the Church, is joined to an adulteress, he is cut off from the promises of the Church. Neither shall he come unto the rewards of Christ who leaves the Church of Christ. He is

---

* Naturrecht and Politik, § 488.

† II. Peter, ii., 7.—II. John, 10.—II. Tim. ii., 25.—Tit. iii., 10, 11.— Gal. i., 8.—I. Tim. i., 19.—II. Thess. ii., 11,

an alien, he is an outcast, he is an enemy. *He can no longer have God for a father, who has not the Church for a mother."* Two centuries later, the Church is called by St. Paulinus, of Nola, "the alone one and the perfect one to her one bride-groom." There can be no question of *religious* or dogmatic *toleration* for the Catholic Church; the very word is an insult to her who represents God on earth. Religious toleration for the Church would be indifferentism to eternal truth, and, as such, something detestable.

Cardinal Hergenroether pointedly says :* "The Catholic Church must, with St. Peter, condemn those who bring in sects of perdition (heretics), lying teachers, who bring upon them-selves swift destruction. She claims, and must claim ever and everywhere as a necessity of her existence, that her doc-trine is of God and of Christ. Wherefore she can admit no right to gainsay the divine revelation entrusted to her, nor even the right to remain indifferent towards it. The propo-sition once established that there is but one true Church, out of which there is no salvation, also the proposition that this church can only be the Roman Catholic Church, man's wel-fare demands that all attempts to withdraw him from the pale of the Church, should be firmly resisted."

When we know a man to be in error, we are not allowed to confirm him in it. It is moreover a duty of charity to point out to him his error. How could the Church let men hope for salvation when they are in error about it? "This attitude," says Hergenroether,† "so natural and so neces-sary, which renders it impossible for the Church to come to terms with other religious opinions and parties, and ren-

*Church and State. 2 Vols., London: Burns & Oates. II. Vol. p. 347.
† l. c., p. 353.

ders her so dear and precious to her children, is precisely
what causes the hatred felt for her by those without her
pale."

God Himself in the Old Law enjoined religious intolerance. The Israelites could not tolerate religious dissent,
and as their religion was intimately connected with all their
civil institutions, death was the penalty for those who
revolted against the Jewish religion.

Let us also state, with the illustrious Hergenoether,*
"that the Church has always recognized that people might
live in error of faith and yet be saved ; that they might be in
unconscious spiritual communion with the true Church,
although through invincible ignorance they were not in
external communion with her ; that condemnation regarded
false *principles*, not the *persons* in error ; that towards these
all the duties of brotherly love were to be exercised, and
that no Catholic had the smallest right to impute guilt to
them."

But now we must necessarily make that most important
distinction which will take away a great deal of the odium
which attaches to the hideous word "intolerance." We
must distinguish between religious or dogmatic, and civil or
political intolerance. "Religious intolerance, which the true
Church firmly maintains, does not necessitate civil intolerance, which would permit no other religion to exist. However convinced one may be of the truth of his own religion,
he may let others live in peace without belonging to it, and
fulfill towards them with zeal and pleasure all the duties of
fraternal love expressly enjoined by the Church."†

* l. c., p. 350.
† Hergenroether, l. c., p. 353.

During the middle ages religion was so bound into the framework of society that to disturb religion was to shake the government in its foundation. Heresy then was a political crime, and operated against the civil law.

Even the Roman jurists, as far back as the fifth century, regarded heresy as an offense against civil society, and the Justinian Code says:* "What is done against the divine religion is an injury to all." Heresy then was considered a graver crime than high treason : " Far more grevious is it to offend the heavenly than the earthly king." Cardinal Hergenroether writes :† " In these days crimes against earthly kings are punished with extremest penalties, but crimes against the Majesty of God are punished scarcely or not at all, and blasphemy, once a capital offense, is disregarded ; and it is very difficult for a mind imbued with these ideas to estimate at their proper value, or in any degree, these ancient laws, once approved universally, and esteemed of undoubted necessity."

But in these our days, unlimited recognition or even toleration of all forms of worship cannot be required of any State. Our free United States must draw the line somewhere. Mormonism is too much even for American toleration.

So long as Europe was Catholic, while the temporal order was united with and subserved the religious, heretics were rebels against society and had to be punished.

Every one will admit that a man has no right to do evil ; neither has he a right to teach and spread evil, to defend and promote error. Lawful authority, according to St. Paul,

* c. I., 5 de haeret.
† l. c., p. 304.

holds the power of punishing evil-doers ; as God's minister for good " it beareth not the sword in vain."*

But the governments of the civilized world have undergone a great change; they are no longer professedly catholic, as in the middle ages ; all sins against religion can no longer be sins against society, and consequently cannot be punished by the State. Thus religious toleration has become a necessity in our modern society. Americans to-day need not boast of tolerance in matters of religion ; it is less an American virtue than a social necessity.

But when, as often happens, Protestants take to themselves the credit of having blessed society with religious liberty, they compel our attention to their history; and this does not bear them out. "Protestantism," as the great American philospher Brownson remarks, " is really in its very nature and essence an earnest and solemn protest against religious liberty."† Religious liberty is defined by the same author as "absolute freedom of religion, in its doctrine, discipline and worship, from all human authority."‡

Religious intolerance, (though the statement seem harsh, the fault is not ours,) is the very life and nature of Protestantism. At the Diet of Spires, held in April, 1529, it was decreed that all religious strife should cease until the next ecumenical council; that those princes who had introduced the "new religion" into their domains might retain and practice it without hindrance ; but that they should *tolerate* the free exercise of the old religion. Against this last clause the Lutheran princes, instructed by their preaçhers, protested, declaring it to be against " God and His Holy Word."

* Cf. Rom. xiii., 1-4.

† Complete Works, XIII., 226.

‡ Ibidim, X., 208.

From this public Protestation against the free exercise of the religion of their Catholic fellow-citizens, the Reformers and their children received the significant name *Protestants*.[*]

Prof. Gammell correctly calls the Protestant Reformation in France and Germany, "an uprising of the human mind against the principle of absolute authority in matters of religion." So it was; the crime of Lucifer; a rebellion of the human mind against the authority of God, which the Church represents on earth.[†] The Reformers rose above divine authority, by claiming more authority than the Church. They interpreted and even altered the Holy Scriptures as they pleased and tolerated no opposition. "Whosoever teaches differently," Luther writes, "from what I have taught, or whosoever condemns, he condemns God and must remain a child of hell."[‡] He claims to have "more power in his little finger than a thousand popes, kings, princes and doctors."

The "principle of absolute authority in matters of religion" once destroyed, what is there left of religion? Protestantism, we say with Brownson,[§] "is the substitution of the temporal for the spiritual, and man for God; in its original form, it was the union of the temporal and spiritual sovereignties in the hands of the temporal prince, that is, the conversion of the spiritual into a temporal authority. . . The history of the introduction and establishment of Protestantism, in the sixteenth century, in what are now called the Protestant nations of Europe, fully confirms the assertion that Protestantism has no religious character properly so

* Janssen, III., 138.
† Luke x., 16.
‡ Saemmtliche Werke, 28, 346.
§ Complete Works, X., 429, 430.

called." Protestantism has no dogmas, (and boasts of it ;) it has but theories; religious views; opinions which daily change and are as numerous as there are Protestant heads : *quot capita, tot sensus.* And yet, strange to say, though in its very nature hostile to true religious liberty, Protestantism clothes itself with the appearance of liberty in the eyes of the world, by favoring the dominant passions and tendencies of the age; by holding "broad views" of Christianity, etc.

Nevertheless, it is an historical fact that, in Europe, Protestantism was the mother of monarchical despotism and imperial absolutism. It was introduced by the strong arm of the secular power, and where it did not obtain the permanent aid of civil power, as in France, it could not be permanently established. The motto of John Knox ran thus : "The institution and transformation of religion belongs to civil authority."

"Religious intolerance," Prof. Gammell remarks, "belongs to human nature and manifests itself in a vast variety of ways." It certainly was a part of the nature of the Reformist Leaders, and truly, indeed, did it manifest itself in a variety of ways.

The father of Protestantism, Martin Luther, was the embodiment of intolerance, civil as well as religious. He first flattered the poor peasants in Germany with promises of liberty, and seduced them to rebellion ; then a few months later he preached their slaughter as if they were so many wild beasts. Of his tract "Against the Murderous and Rapacious Rabble of Peasants," a Protestant writer in the Westminster Review says, it is "the most terrible appeal to bloodshed ever published by a minister of Christ's Church."*

* Jan., 1884.

5

One hundred and fifty thousand peasants*—where is the massacre of St. Bartholomew?—were slain in the peasants' war. Luther afterwards boasted of this slaughter: "I, Martin Luther, have slain all the peasants in the insurrection because I commanded them to be killed; their blood is upon my head."† We shall forbear quoting any of Luther's vile invectives and intolerant expletives against the Church from which he apostatized.

Enough, to recite one passage from his book against the Jews: "These impudent, lying devils ought not to be allowed to praise or pray to God, since their praise, thanksgiving, prayer and teaching is mere blasphemy and idolatry. The penalty for any act of worship on the part of a Jew should be loss of life. Not only all their books, but even the Bible to its last leaf shall be taken from them. Not only are their synagogues to be burnt, but let him, who can, throw pitch and sulphur upon them; if any one could throw hell-fire, it were good, so that God might see our earnestness, and the whole world such an example."‡

Our Protestant friend, in the Westminster Review, is forced to declare the writings of Luther, Melanchton and other Protestants against the early Anabaptists " the quintessence of bigotry and the narrowest theological intolerance."§

Melanchton, the mildest of all the "Reformers," demanded expressly that the Anabaptists should atone for their heresy

---

* Geissel, Kaiserdom, Coeln, 1876, p. 315.

† Saemmtliche Werke, 59, 284.

‡ Saemmtliche Werke, 32. (Cited in Westm. Review, Jan. 1884.) The present Court preacher at Berlin is doing his best to follow the advice of his "apostle."

§ Jan. '84, p. 29.

with death.* He approved of the burning of Servetus as a heretic, and called the hideous deed of Calvin "a pious and memorable example for all posterity."

Zwingli's motto was : "Evangelium sitit sanguinem, (the Gospel thirsts for blood). It was not for having such a motto, but for holding a different *view* on a theological point, that Luther called him "in and in, out and out, through and through, devil-possessed, blasphemous heart, impudent liar."†

And *Calvin*, the father of the Huguenots, whose doctrines, according to Prof. Gammell, "have ever since exercised a controlling influence on the religious thought of at least half of Protestant Christendom,"—called for the establishment of an inquisition that would "extirpate the race of heretics."‡

This "Reformer" was the darkest, the most brutal, cruel and blood-thirsty of them all. Between the years 1542 and 1546, he had something like 900 people arrested as "heretics." He preached an absolute terrorism. During his "apostolic sojourn" at Geneva the prisons could not hold all those who were punished for heresy. The tortures used to force confessions were barbarous ; to escape them, many committed suicide. Even women and children were arrested on mere suspicion ; were tortured and burned with fiery pincers, were buried in dungeons, etc. The arm of the hangman grew weary and unable for its cruel work.§

All who differed in the least from Calvin's opinions were made to feel the wrath of the "Reformer." Let us give a few instances. The preacher *Sebastian Castellio*, who contradicted Calvin's teachings on predestination, was exiled.—

* Corp. Reform. IX., 77.
† See Westm. Review, l. c.
‡ Cf. Galiffe, Nouvelles pages d'Histoire exacte, Geneve, 1862, p. 109.
§ Kampfschutte, Johann Calvin, Leipzig, 1869, p. 424.

Jerome Bolsec, a physician, was thrown into prison and afterwards expelled from Germany for the same reason.—*Pierre Ameaux*, a noble councilman of Geneva, who in a tipsy mood had made fun of Calvin's manner of preaching, was, by the express command of the "Reformer" (though against the will of the city council and the people), forced to do public penance, in his shirt, kneeling on the public street and holding a candle in his hand.—*Francis Favre*, and his fair daughter, the wife of General Perrin, had made merry dancing at a wedding, and for this offense were thrown into prison. General Perrin, indignant at the ill-treatment of his young wife and his father-in-law, used hard language against Calvin, whereupon he was imprisoned, degraded from office and forced to apologize. Later on Perrin had to flee from the anger of the "Reformer," was sentenced to death and burned in effigy.—*James Greut* was beheaded, for having called Calvin a dog an account of his tyranny.—*Michael Servetus*, a Spanish physician, who disagreed with Calvin on the doctrine of the Blessed Trinity, was burned to death. To justify this execution, Calvin wrote a pamphlet entitled: "*Fidelis expositio errorum Mich. Serveti et brevis eorum refutatio, ubi docetur, jure gladii coërcendos esse hereticos.*"

It was not enough for Calvin, the man of "free inquiry" and of "the pure Gospel," to exercise in all directions, during his stay in Geneva, the worst absolutism and terrorism ; he extended his cruel attempts to England and besought the Duke of Somerset, the Regent of England, to destroy with the sword all those, particularly Catholics, who dared to oppose the Reform Church of England.*

Henry VIII., the "Reformer" of England, put to death

* Kirche oder Protestantismus, Mainz, 1883, p. 60.

not less than 30,000 Englishmen for their faith; and Cranmer justified his butcheries by texts from Holy Scripture.

And what shall we say of Protestant tyranny in Catholic Ireland? The very thought of it must fill the heart with horror.

Speaking of the violent introduction of Protestantism into England under Queen Elizabeth, the Protestant historian Cobbett says:* "Talk about Catholic persecution and cruelty! Where are you to find persecution and cruelty like this? Elizabeth put, in one way or another, more Catholics to death, in one year, *for not becoming apostates* to the religion which she had sworn to be hers, and to be the only true one, than Mary put to death in her whole reign for having apostatized from the religion of her and their fathers, and to which religion she herself had always adhered. Yet, the former is called, or has been called, good Queen Bess, and the latter bloody Queen Mary. Even the horrid massacre of St. Bartholomew was nothing, when fairly compared with the butcheries and other cruelties of the reign of this Protestant Queen of England; yes, a mere nothing; and yet she put on mourning on that occasion, and had the consummate hypocrisy to affect horror at the cruelties that the king of France had committed."

Between the years 1660 and 1685, 25,000 persons were imprisoned for their faith, in England, and 1,500 families were ruined for the same cause.†

Maryland, the "cradle of religious liberty," was settled by persecuted English Catholics. They were the first colony in the United States to grant full toleration in religious matters; and "the happiness of the Colony," as Prof. Bancroft

* W. Cobbett, Protestant Reformation, New York: Sadlier & Co., p. 143.
† See Mackintosh, History of the English Revolution.

says, "was enviable. The persecuted and the unhappy thronged to the domains of the benevolent prince (Baltimore) . . . . The children of misfortune sought protection under the tolerant sceptre of the Roman Catholic."* Scarcely had Protestants obtained control of the Legislature, when with base ingratitude they deprived their Catholic brethren of the protection of the law. Thus, as Bancroft remarks, " Roman Catholics were disfranchised in the province which they had planted."†

In Massachusetts, the cold and relentless Puritans made death the penalty for a Jesuit who should enter the colony.

The Blue Laws of Connecticut had a statute that "no priest shall abide in this dominion ; he shall be banished and suffer death on his return. Priests may be seized by any one without a warrant."‡

In Protestant Mecklenburg, Catholics, at the present day, are forbidden the free exercise of their religion.

And what shall we say of the fearful persecution of Roman Catholics under the first Protestant Emperor in Germany ? A persecution, though less sanguinary, yet more diabolical than that under the Roman Cesars against the early Christians !

According to Prof. Gammell, the social organization of Rhode Island has made "persecutors like Catherine de Medicis and Louis. XIV. no longer possible in civilized nations." What about the Protestant Chancellor of the Protestant Emperor,—what about Bismark and the Kulturkampf ? Did Prof. Gammell read the latest development of the dream of Bismark's life, his infernal scheme against Catholic Poland ?

---

* History of the United States, Vol. I.—(The author's last Revision).
† Ibidem, p. 440.
‡ Cf. Barber's Antiquities of New Haven.

And by the way, when will the light of liberty of worship dawn upon the inmates of the State Reform Schools for boys and girls in Rhode Island?

There have been Catholic sovereigns who have persecuted heretics for political and state purposes. The Catholic Church is not to be blamed for it ; for she never approved of it. In religion God demands man's free will, the voluntary sacrifice of obedience, the ready submission of man to His divine law. Hence the Church never compelled any one to receive her faith. Where people were compelled to Catholic worship, it was against the will and without the authority of the Church.

There is another fact to which we beg to call attention ; Catholics have never persecuted Protestants for being Protestants, but for falling away from the Church of God, for blaspheming divine truth, for seducing others to like acts, and for subverting social order. Protestants, however, have persecuted Catholics for being Catholics, and for remaining faithful to the religion of their fathers.

APPENDIX.

VERNACULAR VERSIONS MADE IN SEVERAL EUROPEAN
TONGUES DURING THE SIXTY OR SEVENTY YEARS IMMEDI-
ATELY PRECEDING THE REFORMATION.

Versions in High German.

1462–6 A. D., probably at Strassburg, by Eggestein.

c. 1466 A. D., without name of place.

1470–5 A. D., probably at Augsburg.

1470–3 A. D., either at Nuremberg or Basel.

1473–5 A. D., at Augsburg.

1477 A. D., at Augsburg.

1477 A. D., at Augsburg.

1480 A. D., at Augsburg.

1483 A. D., at Nuremberg, by A. Koburger.

(A real édition de luxe, beautifully illustrated with over one
hundred wood-cuts by the celebrated Michael Wohlgemuth.)

1485 A. D., at Strassburg.

1487 A. D., at Augsburg.

1490 A. D., at Augsburg.

1507 A. D., at Augsburg.

1518 A. D., at Augsburg.

1524 A. D., at Augsburg.

Versions in Low German.

No date,* at Cologne.
No date, at Cologne.
1477 A. D., at Delft.
1494 A. D., at Lübeck.
1522 A. D., at Halberstadt.   Besides the complete editions of the Bible in High and Low German, versions of parts of the Holy Scriptures were numerous.   There appeared up to the year 1513 eleven editions of the Psalms, and up to 1518 twenty-five editions of the Epistles and Gospels in German.

Æthiopian Version.

1513 A. D. The Psalms, and the Canticle of Canticles, printed by Potken, in Rome.

Slavish Versions.

1481 A. D. Psalterion ; printed at Cracow.
1491 A. D. Psalterion ; printed at Cracow.
1495 A. D. Psalterion ; printed at Cetynia.
1499 A. D. A complete Bible, in manuscript.
1512 A. D. Evangelarion.

Polish Versions.

1455 A. D. A complete Bible, translated by the Vicar Andreas de Jasowicz and copied by Peter de Radoszyc ; at Korczyn.

1514 A. D. The Gospel of St. John ; printed by Haller, in Cracow.

1522 A. D. The books of Solomon ; printed by Wietor, in Cracow.

* The first printed books had neither a date nor name of place.

Czech Versions.

There are yet extant thirty-three manuscripts of complete Bibles, and twenty-eight of the New Testament, from the fifteenth century.

1475 A. D. The New Testament; printed at Pilsen.

1480 A. D. The New Testament; printed at Pilsen.

1487 A. D. The Psalter; printed at Prague.

1488 A. D. The complete Bible; printed at Prague.

1489 A. D. The complete Bible; printed at Kuttenberg.

1498 A. D. The New Testament; printed at Prague.

1499 A. D. The Psalter; printed at Pilsen.

1506 A. D. The complete Bible; printed at Venice.

1508 A. D. The Psalter; printed at Pilsen.

1513 A. D. The New Testament; printed at Prague.

Italian Version.

• 1471 A. D. The complete Bible, by the Camaldulensian monk, Nicholas de Malermi. This Bible appeared in *nine* editions before the close of the fifteenth century, and in twelve more editions during the following century.

Spanish Version.

1478 A. D. The complete Bible, by the Carthusian general, Boniface Ferrer.

French Versions.

1474 A. D. The Psalter.

c. 1478 A. D. The Bible of Julien, as it is called (Le Nou veau Test. et la declaration dicelluy faicte et composée par Julien Macho et Pierre Farget. Lyon: B. Buyer. And Les livres de l'Ancien Test., histoires en François). Two editions.

1482 A. D. Several books of the Old Testament.

1484 A. D. The edition of Menand.

1487 A. D. The complete Bible, translated by J. de Rely, confessor to King Charles VIII.; printed at Paris by Verard; two folios. This Bible appeared in several editions.

1502 A. D. The Apocalypse.

1507 A. D. The Epistles of St. Paul.

1513 A. D. The Psalms.

1523 A. D. The version from the Vulgate, by Le Fèvre d'Estaples.

Hungarian Versions.

Versions were made into the Hungarian language long before the fifteenth century. A Version of the complete Bible was made by the monk Bathory, who died in 1456.

Of the greatest importance for the instruction and edification of the people were those popular books called Postillen (from the initial words, "post illa verba"), or Plenarien ("plenarium," the whole Gospel), which contained the epistles and gospels for the Sundays of the year, with brief glosses and explanations, many of them containing a German translation of the Mass and also liturgical commentaries on the divine service. Dr. Falk gives a full and accurate list of ninety-nine Postillen up to 1520 which are yet kept in different libraries.*

These Postillen, of which many were written in excellent German, contained the pure, unchangeable teachings of the Church and were powerful instructors of the Christian fam-

* Druckkunst, pp. 80–83.

ily. Götze, a Protestant author, candidly confesses: "When one considers that a Latin missal was in use even in the smallest church, while these Gospel-books could only be used by the laity for private devotions, the number of the latter is an extraordinarily large one, and attests the eagerness of the German people to have the word of God brought home to them in their mother-tongue. They were not content merely to assist bodily at divine service, but they longed for the spiritual food of the word of God. For these books, which from their magnificent size could not have been cheap, were undoubtedly purchased only by those who seriously wished to study and understand the divine word."*

Vernacular Versions in England.

Blunt thinks† that English divines have always shown a greater interest in translations of the Bible into the vernacular than the divines of any other European nation.

As early as the seventh century the monk Caedmon composed a Bible History in Anglo-Saxon, containing the principal events of the Old and New Testament.

In the eighth century St. Aldhelm, bishop of Sherborn, translated the Psalms; Bishop Cadfrid, of Lindisfarne, a considerable portion of the Scriptures; the Venerable Bede the whole Bible.

In the ninth century King Alfred translated a great part of the Psalter; a version of the Gospels was made by the priest Aldredus; a second version of the Gospels by Owun and Foerman.

In the tenth century the learned priest Aelfric translated the Pentateuch, Judith, Job and other books of the Old Tes-

* Dr. Falk, Druckkunst, p. 30.
† History of the Reformation in England.

tament. Sirgwerd, a nobleman, wrote a compendium of the Old and New Testament.

Not quite a hundred years after the Norman conquest the Psalms were turned into English; and Samson de Nantueil wrote a paraphrase of the book of Proverbs.

About the year 1200 a translation of the whole Bible was published. In the middle of the thirteenth century a translation of the complete Bible; towards the end of this century a metrical translation of the Psalms.

From the fourteenth century: a version of the Psalms by William de Shorham; another by the Augustinian, Richard Roll.

The chaplain of Lord Thomas de Berkley, John Trevisa, translated the whole Bible either contemporaneously with or before Wycliff.*

With these facts before him, John Fox, in his Preface to "the Gospels of the fower Evangelists translated into the vulgare toung of the Saxons," etc, 1571, remarks: "If histories will be examined well, we shall finde both before the conquest and after as well before John Wicliffe was borne, as since the whole body of Scriptures by sundry men translated into this our country tongue."

* For reference see " Der Katholik." Zeitschrift, Mainz. Vol 52, p. 72— p. 89, New series.

CPSIA information can be obtained
at www.ICGtesting.com
Printed in the USA
BVHW061140270219
541296BV00021B/1358/P